D0842674

I Heard a Sound

Text copyright © 2020 by David J. Ward

Illustrations copyright © 2020 by Eric Comstock

All Rights Reserved

Book design by Eric Comstock

HOLIDAY HOUSE is registered in the U.S. Patent and Trademark Office.

Printed and bound in April 2020 at Toppan Leefung, DongGuan City, China.

The artwork was created with digital tools.

www.holidayhouse.com

First Edition

1 3 5 7 9 10 8 6 4 2

Library of Congress Cataloging-in-Publication Data

Names: Ward, David J., author. | Comstock, Eric, illustrator.

Title: I heard a sound / David J Ward, Eric Comstock.

Description: New York City : Holiday House, [2020] | Audience: Ages 6–9

Audience: Grades 2–3 | Summary: "Learn the science of sound with easy

experiments and examples from everyday life"—Provided by publisher.

Identifiers: LCCN 2019049889 | ISBN 9780823437047 (hardcover)

Subjects: LCSH: Sounds—Juvenile literature.

Classification: LCC QC225.5 .W37 2020 | DDC 534—dc23

LC record available at https://lccn.loc.gov/2019049889

I Heard a Sound

by David J. Ward

illustrated by Eric Comstock

HOLIDAY HOUSE   NEW YORK

It came from that bike.

Look! A card is on the spokes. When the wheel spins, the card hits the spokes. The card moves back and forth very fast. The card is **vibrating**. The spokes are vibrating too. That is what makes the sound.

Chirp Chirp

I heard another **sound.**

Did you hear that one?

LET'S see what made it.

6

A cricket made that sound! How does it do that? It rubs its wings together. Its wings vibrate. That is what makes the sound. Sounds come from vibrating things.

Have you ever played with

Do you have one around?

Hold one end of the spring toy. Have someone else hold the other end. Stretch the spring toy across a smooth floor. Now push your end without letting go. See how your push moves through the spring toy?

Push lots of times! You are making push waves! Sound is a push wave too. It moves through the air like your waves in the spring toy.

a spring toy?

When a card flaps on a bike spoke, it pushes the air around it. When cricket wings vibrate, they push the air too. They make push waves in the air.

The waves move through the air. They can move all the way to your ears. When the sound waves get to your ears, you hear them!

9

Say

When I talk, my throat vibrates. I can feel it with my hand. Your throat will do it too! Put your hand on the front of your throat.

Now talk.

Sound.

Can you feel that?

The sound comes from your throat. You have two small flaps in there called **vocal cords.** When you speak, they vibrate. That is what makes the sound of your voice.

Vocal Cords

Do you want to see how your **vocal cords** work? You can make something like them. Here is how to do it:

WHAT YOU WILL NEED
Scissors, a balloon, and a cardboard tube

1. Ask an adult to help.

2. Cut a slit in the round end of the balloon.

3. Cut off the end of the balloon.

4. Stretch the balloon over the end of the tube. Make sure the slit is over the hole. Stretch it tight!

5. Now put the other end around your mouth. Blow hard into the tube. The balloon makes a sound!

When you blow, air goes through the slit. The slit vibrates. That is what your vocal cords do!

Look what I can do!

LET GO

I can make a sound
with this ruler.
I can make it vibrate.
I pull down, then let go.

See the ruler bounce?
It is vibrating!

14

Do you want to try? It's fun!

Now slide more of the ruler off the table. Pull down, and let go! The ruler does not bounce as fast. The sound is different too. The sound is lower.

Now try with less of the ruler off the table. The ruler bounces faster! The sound is higher than before. When things vibrate quickly, they sound high. When things vibrate slowly, they sound low.

A big bell makes a low sound.
A little bell makes a high sound.
A big drum? It sounds low.
A little drum? It sounds high.
Guess why!

BOOM

Answer:

They do not vibrate the same.

Big things

vibrate slowly, so they sound low.

Little things

vibrate quickly, so they sound high.

Most big people have big vocal cords.
That makes their voices lower.

Most small people have small vocal cords.
That makes their voices higher.

Big = Low

Little = High

squeak

Do you have

If you do, tie it to a table or chair. Now pull the string tight and hold it with one hand. With your other hand, pluck the string.

Pull it up and let go.

It makes a sound! The string is vibrating. Now hold the string so it is shorter.

Pull it tight!

Pluck the string again. The sound is different! The sound is higher than before. When the string is long, it vibrates slowly. When the string is short, it vibrates quickly.

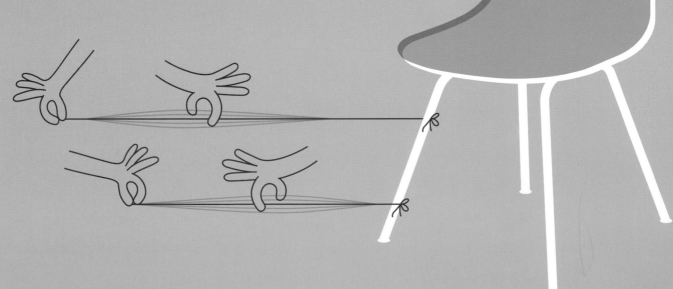

any string?

That is how a guitar works! The musician plucks a string. The string vibrates.

Do you have a straw?

You can make a sound with it. Blow into the straw. Blow without putting your mouth on it. It makes a sound! Something is vibrating. But what could it be? Is it the straw?

No. It is the air inside. The air inside is vibrating! We cannot see it, but it is. When you blow, the air inside wiggles back and forth a little. That is what makes the sound.

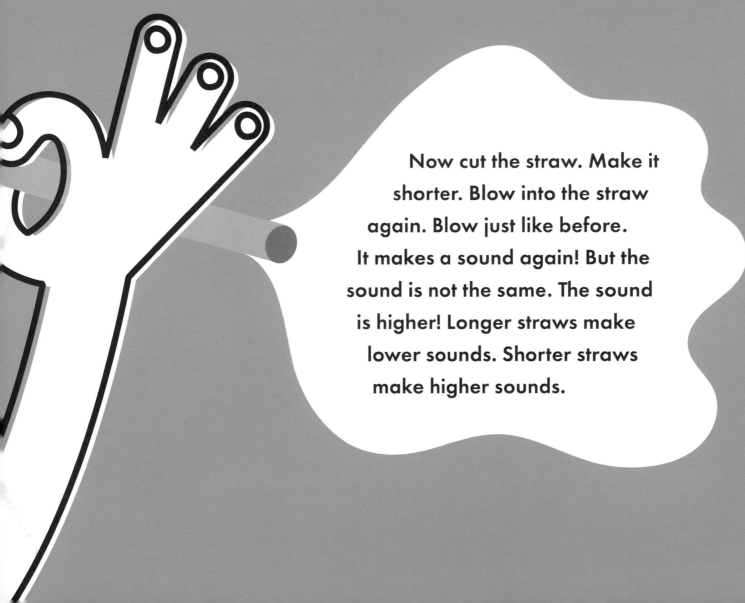

Now cut the straw. Make it shorter. Blow into the straw again. Blow just like before. It makes a sound again! But the sound is not the same. The sound is higher! Longer straws make lower sounds. Shorter straws make higher sounds.

clarinet

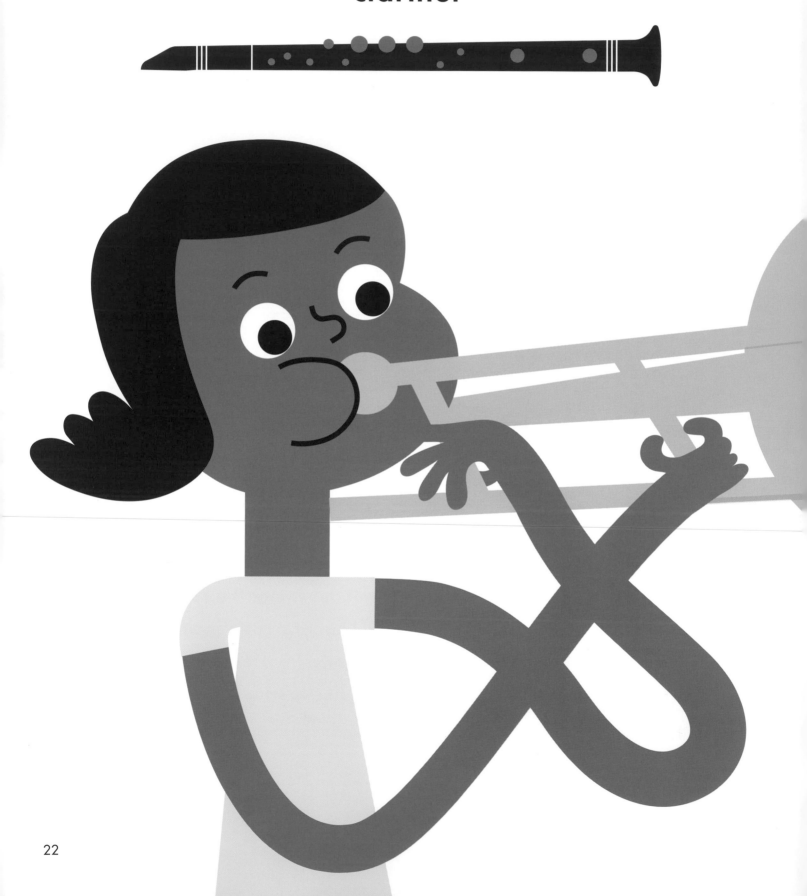

Many musical instruments work that way.
The musician blows into the instrument. The air inside
vibrates. That is what makes the sound. Flutes work
that way. So do clarinets. Flutes and clarinets are tubes
with holes. Covering the holes changes the sound.

Trombones are tubes too. The musician blows into the tube.
She vibrates her lips while she blows. That vibrates the air
inside. She can make the tube longer by sliding her arm out.
The longer tube makes a lower sound!

You can make a musical instrument!

WHAT YOU WILL NEED

Four straws, scissors,

a craft stick, and tape or glue

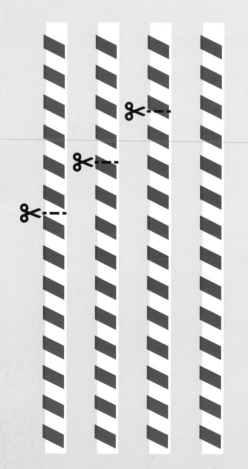

1. Ask an adult to help.

2. Cut each straw a different length.

3. Lay them side-by-side, tall to short.
    Use all seven pieces.

4. Tape or glue them to the craft stick.

You made a pan flute!

Blow across each straw. Blow without putting your mouth on the straws.

Each straw makes a different sound!

Can you play a song?

Sound comes from vibrating things.

But sound can also make things vibrate.

Do you want to see how?

You will need a piece of wax paper. Cover your mouth with the wax paper. Now make a loud sound into the wax paper. Just yell or say "Aaaah!" What did you hear?

Did the wax paper buzz? Your voice is making it vibrate! The vibrating paper makes a sound. It might even tickle your lips! Your voice can make other things vibrate too.

That's how a string telephone works. Have you ever made one? It is easy! Do you want to try? You will be able to talk to a friend through a piece of string.

Aaaah!

You can make a string telephone!

WHAT YOU WILL NEED: Pencil, two paper cups, string, and tape

1. Use the pencil to poke a small hole in the bottom of each cup.

2. Put the string through the bottom of one cup.

3. Tape the end of the string to the inside of the cup.

4. Now put the other end of the string through the bottom of the other cup.

5. Tape the string inside the second cup.

6. Hold one cup. Give the other cup to a friend.

7. Pull the string tight! It needs to be tight to work.

8. Put the cup by your ear.

9. Have your friend speak into the other cup.

Hi, friend.

Can you hear your friend? The sound vibrations go through the string. You can talk to each other using the string telephone. Sound can travel through all kinds of things!

Can you go through a wall?

No.
Neither can I.

But sound ~~~~~~~~~~ can!

Sound can travel through all kinds of things.

Want to hear that?

Find a hard floor. Put your ear on the floor. Cover your other ear. Have your friend go to the other side of the room.

Now have your friend tap on the floor. Could you hear the tap? The sound traveled through the floor!

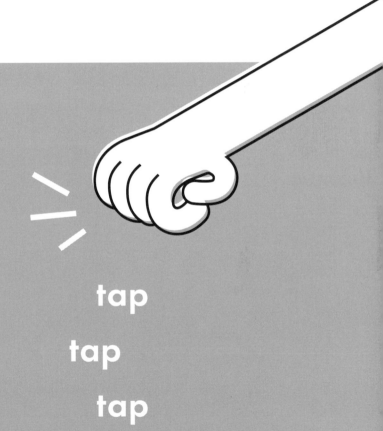

tap

tap

tap

Sound can go through water too.

That is how whales talk to each other. You can do it too. You can yell to a friend underwater. Your voice will sound funny. But your friend will hear it. Maybe a whale will hear it too!

Hello, whale!

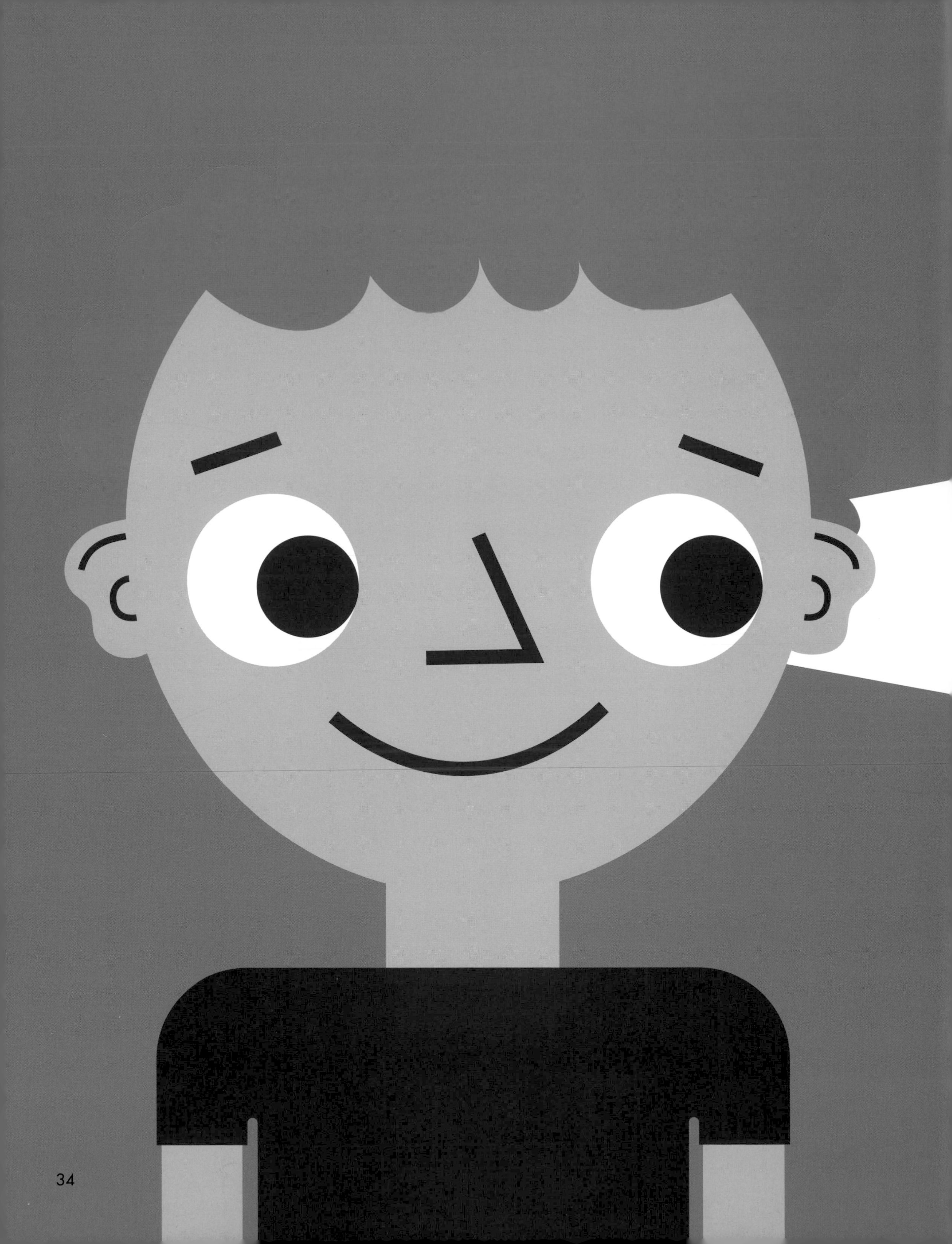

Have you ever looked at someone's ear?

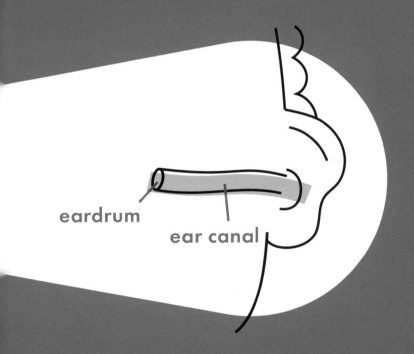

eardrum

ear canal

Look closely. There is a hole in there. Do you see it? Deep inside the hole is something called an eardrum. It is too deep inside there for you to see. It is a very thin piece of skin that stretches across the hole.

Your ears have eardrums too. When sound goes into your ears, it makes your eardrums vibrate. When your eardrums vibrate, your brain gets a signal. That is how your brain knows there is a sound. That is how you hear!

Wee-ooo! Wee-ooo! Wee-ooo!

Your ears are amazing! You can hear fireworks. You also can hear a tiny whisper. You can hear a police car siren. And you can hear the sound of wind in the trees. Hearing different sounds is fun!

So take care of your ears. Don't ever put anything inside your ears. You could hurt your eardrums!
Very loud sounds can hurt your eardrums too. So cover your ears when loud sounds are around.

Listen! Did you hear that?

m e o w

Fire

There are so many things to hear. Cat meows and car horns. Firetrucks and frogs. Sawing logs. Singing birds. Crunching leaves. Cheering crowds. And a marching band in the parade. All those sounds come from vibrating things.

I heard a sound!
What do you hear?

Glossary

Ear canal: The small tunnel in the middle of your ear. Each of your ear canals leads to an eardrum.

Eardrum: The very thin piece of skin that stretches across your ear canal. It vibrates when it is hit by a sound vibration.

Musician: A person who plays music.

Signal: A message that your ears send to your brain. The messages travel through nerves. The messages tell your brain what kind of sound you are hearing.

Sound: Tiny vibrations that our ears can sense.

Sound wave: A pushing motion that can travel through air, liquids (such as water), and solids (such as wood or concrete). Sound waves are made by vibrating objects.

Vibrate: To wiggle back and forth.

Vibration: A back-and-forth motion. If an object wiggles back and forth fast enough, it will make a sound we can hear.

Vocal cords: Two folds in the muscle of your throat that vibrate. When they vibrate, they make the sound of your voice. Your vocal cords are at the top of a pipe that comes from your lungs. When you breathe out, air goes past your vocal cords and can make them vibrate.